FRUSTRATION
When Expectations Don't Match Reality

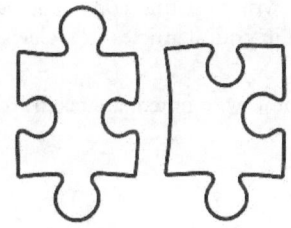

LATONYA STERLING

Frustration
When Expectations Don't Match Reality
By Latonya Sterling

Copyright © 2025 Latonya Sterling
All rights reserved.

No part of this book may be reproduced, stored in a retrieval system, or transmitted in any form or by any means—electronic, mechanical, photocopying, recording, or otherwise—without the prior written permission of the publisher, except in the case of brief quotations embodied in critical articles or reviews.

Scripture quotations, unless otherwise noted, are taken from the ESV. Used by permission. All rights reserved.

ISBN: 9798999589750

First Edition

Cover design generated ChatGPT

Published by Latonya LSimmons Sterling

Contact: latonyasterling@gmail.com

Printed in the United States of America

Table of Contents

Introduction   1

Chapter 1. Moses at the Rock   5
When Leaders Misstep Out of Frustration

Chapter 2. Jonah, Naaman, and Potiphar's Wife   9
Case Studies of Unmet Expectations

Chapter 3. Tracking Frustration   13
Getting to the Root Instead of Dwelling on the Surface

Chapter 4. Frustration at Home   19
Marriage and Family Dynamics

Chapter 5. Frustration at Work   25
Learning to Trust God in the Workplace

Chapter 6. Frustration in the Church   31
When Spiritual Expectations Collide

Chapter 7. God Is Not Like Us   37
Why We Can't Project Human Irritation onto Him

Chapter 8. The Flood, the Wilderness, & the Temple   41
God's Discipline as Love

Chapter 9. Faith Over Frustration   47
Surrendering Expectations

Conclusion – Living Beyond Frustration   51

Introduction

Frustration …we've all felt it. It creeps in when what we hoped for doesn't happen, when people didn't do what we thought they would, or when life simply refuses to cooperate with our plans.

Frustration can be understood on several levels. According to *Merriam-Webster's Collegiate Dictionary*, the simple definition of frustration is "the feeling of being upset, irritated, or disappointed when something doesn't happen the way you expected or desired." A deeper way to put it is this: frustration is the emotional response to the gap between expectation and reality. It rises when our plans, goals, or standards are blocked or unmet.

From a biblical perspective, frustration often reveals that our expectations are misaligned, either with God's will, with the limitations of others, or with the reality of life itself. Left unchecked, frustration can lead us to anger, discouragement, or wrong choices. A powerful example of this is found in Numbers 20, when Moses struck the rock in anger instead of speaking to it as God commanded (Numbers 20:7–12, ESV).

I know this feeling all too well. As a mother, I raised three daughters. I poured myself into teaching them what I believed was right before God. I gave them what I thought was wise counsel, instruction, and truth — everything I thought would guide them into making godly choices. My expectation was simple: because I had taught them, they would follow my teaching. But reality didn't look like that. Like many children, they chose their own paths, made their own mistakes, and sometimes landed in places I never wanted for them.

I was frustrated. My thoughts sounded like this: "After everything I poured into you, how could you not listen? I have taught you better than this. I told you what would happen if you went that way." My frustration wasn't just about their choices. It was about my expectations. I expected my words to guarantee their obedience. I expected my teaching to automatically take root in their hearts. When those expectations didn't meet reality, I was left staring at disappointment.

Later in life, God met me in that place of frustration. He showed me something I'll never forget: "You were frustrated because you were looking at what you did, not at what I was doing. Your job was to plant seeds. Your job was to water. My job is always to bring the increase" (1 Corinthians 3:6, ESV). That revelation shifted my perspective *from control to trust*. I realized that frustration often reveals where I'm clinging to outcomes I was never meant to determine. My job was never to make the seed grow — only to faithfully plant and water.

That's the heart of this book. We live in a world full of expectations — in our families, our marriages, our workplaces, even in our churches. When those expectations don't match reality, frustration comes. However, frustration doesn't have to control us. It can be a signal, a teacher, and even a doorway into deeper trust in God.

In the chapters ahead, we'll look at biblical stories of people who let frustration push them into wrong choices. We'll talk about real-life situations where frustration shows up in parenting, in marriage, on the job, and in church. We'll also learn how to trace frustration back to its source, so we can surrender our expectations to God, and find peace in His will.

Most importantly, we'll see that God is not like us. We often project our human emotions onto Him assuming He must be frustrated, irritated, or disappointed with us the way we get with others. But the truth is, His discipline flows from love, not irritation. His justice is purposeful, not reactionary. His perspective sees the end from the beginning.

My prayer is that this book helps you not only to understand frustration but to walk free from it. I am not here to push my way of thinking onto you. Ultimately, every believer must hear from God for themselves. What I share in these pages are lessons God has shown me, truths that have helped me release frustration and lean more fully on Him. These insights may serve as tools, but it is the Holy Spirit who does the real work in your heart. My hope is simply that as you read you will find encouragement, perspective, and perhaps even a few keys that help you eliminate unnecessary frustration as you learn, like I have, to trust God more deeply.

Chapter 1: Moses at the Rock
When Leaders Misstep Out of Frustration

Moses was a man uniquely chosen by God, a prophet unlike any other in Israel's history. Scripture tells us that "the Lord used to speak to Moses face to face, as a man speaks to his friend" (Exodus 33:11, ESV). He led a nation out of slavery, parted the Red Sea, and stood in God's presence on Mount Sinai. Yet even Moses, humble, faithful, and deeply anointed, was not immune to frustration. The story of Moses striking the rock in Numbers 20 is one of the clearest examples in the Bible of how frustration can lead even the strongest leaders into disobedience.

The people of Israel were once again complaining in the wilderness. They had no water, and their words revealed not only their thirst but also their unbelief. "Why have you made us come up out of Egypt to bring us to this evil place? It is no place for grain or figs or vines or pomegranates, and there is no water to drink" (Numbers 20:5, ESV). This was not the first time they had grumbled, nor would it be the last. For decades Moses had listened to their murmuring, endured their rebellion, and carried the burden of their discontent. By this point in the story, Moses was not just tired. He was worn down, exasperated, and frustrated.

In response to the people's complaint, God gave Moses a clear and specific instruction: "Take the staff, and assemble the congregation, you and Aaron your brother, and tell the rock before their eyes to yield its water. So, you shall bring water out of the rock for them and give drink to the congregation and their cattle" (Numbers 20:8, ESV). The command was simple: speak to the rock. God intended to demonstrate His holiness and His power in a new way, not by repeating the act of striking, as He had once instructed earlier in Exodus 17, but by speaking His word over the rock. Moses, overwhelmed by years of disappointment and irritation, let his frustration take the lead. Instead of speaking to the rock, he rebuked the people: "Hear now, you rebels: shall we bring water for you out of this rock?" (Numbers 20:10, ESV). In anger, he lifted his hand and struck the rock twice with his staff. Water flowed abundantly, and the people drank, but Moses had disobeyed God's command.

God's response was immediate and sobering. "Because you did not believe in me, to uphold me as holy in the eyes of the people of Israel, therefore you shall not bring this assembly into the land that I have given them" (Numbers 20:12, ESV). Frustration had cost Moses dearly. It did not erase his calling or his relationship with God, but it limited his reward. His outburst misrepresented God to the people, turning what should have been a moment of mercy and holiness into a display of irritation and self-focus.

When we look closely at this story, we see how frustration works. First, frustration builds quietly over time. For Moses, it was not just one moment of irritation but years of unresolved strain. Second, frustration shifts our focus away from God and onto ourselves or others. Notice that Moses said, "Shall we bring water for you out of this rock?" (Numbers

20:10, ESV). His words placed the weight of the miracle on himself and Aaron, rather than on God, whose power alone could provide the water. Third, frustration distorts obedience. God had said "speak," but Moses "struck." This was disobedience driven by emotion. Finally, frustration misrepresents God's character. God wanted to show His patience and His holiness to the people, but Moses' anger painted Him as harsh and reactive.

The lesson for us is sobering but also hopeful. Frustration is not harmless. It can distort our actions, misrepresent God to others, and even keep us from stepping fully into or delaying what God intends for us. Yet Moses' story also reminds us that God's plans are never thwarted by human weakness. The water still flowed from the rock. The people still drank. God's mercy still reached them, because ultimately His provision is not dependent on human perfection.

For us, the challenge is not to imagine a life free from frustration but to recognize it quickly and surrender it to God. When we are honest about our limits, when we lay down our control, and when we obey God's word even when our emotions are screaming otherwise, we uphold Him as holy before others. Moses' misstep shows us the danger of giving in to frustration, but it also points us back to the One who never fails, never lashes out in irritation, and never misrepresents His own nature.

Latonya Sterling

Chapter 2: Jonah, Naaman, and Potiphar's Wife Case Studies of Unmet Expectations

Frustration shows up in different ways depending on the person and the situation. Sometimes it reveals itself in sulking, sometimes in anger, and sometimes in manipulation. Scripture gives us multiple examples of how unmet expectations can trigger frustration that leads to wrong choices. Three striking case studies are found in the lives of Jonah, Naaman, and Potiphar's wife.

Jonah's story is one of the clearest biblical portraits of a prophet consumed by frustration. God sent Jonah to Nineveh, a city known for its violence and wickedness, with a message of repentance. To Israel, Nineveh represented more than just another sinful city. It was part of the Assyrian Empire, infamous for brutality, oppression, and acts of terror against conquered peoples. Within a century of Jonah's mission, Assyria would conquer the northern kingdom of Israel and carry its people into exile (2 Kings 17:5–6, ESV). For Jonah, God's call to preach to Nineveh felt like being asked to show compassion to Israel's worst enemy.

When the Ninevites responded to God's warning and repented, Jonah was not happy. Scripture says, "But it displeased Jonah exceedingly, and he was angry. And he prayed to the Lord and said, 'O Lord, is not this what I said when I was yet in my country? That is why I made haste to flee to Tarshish; for I knew that you are a gracious God and merciful, slow to anger and abounding in steadfast love, and relenting from disaster'" (Jonah 4:1–2, ESV). Jonah's expectation was that God would destroy Nineveh. His reality was that God extended mercy. The gap between Jonah's expectation and God's will produced frustration so deep that Jonah sulked outside the city, angry enough to die (Jonah 4:3–5, ESV). Jonah teaches us that frustration can expose a heart more committed to personal preferences than to God's purposes. Jonah lacked mercy, and mercilessness can breed frustration.

Naaman's story provides another example of frustration rooted in unmet expectations. Naaman was a commander of the army of Syria, highly regarded but afflicted with leprosy. When he sought healing through the prophet Elisha, he expected a dramatic display of power. Elisha sent a messenger with a simple instruction: "Go and wash in the Jordan seven times, and your flesh shall be restored, and you shall be clean" (2 Kings 5:10, ESV). Naaman's response was anger. "But Naaman was angry and went away, saying, 'Behold, I thought that he would surely come out to me and stand and call upon the name of the Lord his God, and wave his hand over the place and cure the leper. Are not Abana and Pharpar, the rivers of Damascus, better than all the waters of Israel? Could I not wash in them and be clean?' So he turned and went away in a rage" (2 Kings 5:11–12, ESV).

Naaman's expectation was for a prophet to put on a show worthy of his status, perhaps something that would stroke his pride. Reality was humbler and simpler: wash in the muddy waters of the Jordan. His frustration nearly cost him his healing. Only when his servants urged him to humble himself and follow Elisha's instruction did he obey, and "his flesh was restored like the flesh of a little child, and he was clean" (2 Kings 5:14, ESV). Naaman teaches us that frustration often comes when God's ways do not match our sense of dignity or grandeur. Healing was available, but his lack of humility and expectation of how it should happen nearly blocked the blessing.

Potiphar's wife offers a different picture altogether — one of frustration turning into manipulation and deception. When Joseph was sold into slavery and placed in Potiphar's household, Scripture tells us that Joseph was "handsome in form and appearance" (Genesis 39:6, ESV). Potiphar's wife attempted to seduce him, but Joseph refused, saying, "How then can I do this great wickedness and sin against God?" (Genesis 39:9, ESV). Day after day she pursued him, and day after day he refused. Eventually, her unmet desire produced frustration that exploded into a false accusation. When Joseph fled her advances, she cried out, accusing him of assault, and Joseph was thrown into prison (Genesis 39:11–20, ESV).

Potiphar's wife's frustration reveals another angle. When expectations are rooted in sin, their disappointment breeds destructive behavior. Unlike Jonah, whose expectation clashed with God's mercy, or Naaman, whose pride resisted God's humility, Potiphar's wife allowed her unmet desire to twist into manipulation. Her story reminds us that frustration unchecked by truth can become a weapon that damages not only ourselves but also the innocent.

Together, Jonah, Naaman, and Potiphar's wife illustrate three faces of frustration. Jonah shows us the sulking heart that cannot accept God's will. Naaman shows us the proud heart that resists God's humble methods. Potiphar's wife shows us the manipulative heart that lashes out when sinful desires are denied. Each story underscores the same truth. Frustration is not neutral. Left unaddressed, it can pull us away from God's purposes, blind us to His mercy, and lead us into harmful choices.

Chapter 3: Tracking Frustration
Getting to the Root Instead of
Dwelling on the Surface

Frustration rarely appears out of nowhere. It usually points to something deeper than the situation in front of us. The argument with a spouse, the child who won't listen, the job that feels unfair — these are often symptoms rather than causes. To track frustration means to look beneath the surface irritation and uncover what is really happening. It means asking not only *what* happened, but *why* it affected us the way it did.

Sometimes, we honestly believe we are operating in God's will when, in reality, we are projecting our own standards onto others. Those standards may sound godly, and they may even be good, but if God has not required them of someone else, we cannot hold them to it. It is easy to confuse personal convictions with divine commands. When we do, frustration often follows. This does not mean the standard itself is wrong. It simply means we must be careful not to impose expectations God has not given us the authority to enforce.

I saw having wrong expectations clearly in my own life when I was once engaged to be married. I met a man in church who was a believer, and I was initially drawn to the way he spoke about the Word of God. For a season, it appeared that the Word was shaping his life, and I began to form expectations about our future. In my mind, the direction seemed obvious. I expected marriage. I expected growth. I expected a shared spiritual journey.

Over time, however, reality began to diverge from what I had imagined. I noticed attitudes and behaviors that concerned me, but because I was already emotionally invested, I minimized what I saw. I reasoned it away. I held onto what I believed *should* be instead of honestly facing what *was*. When the relationship eventually ended — and he was the one who ended it — I was overwhelmed with frustration. I was hurt, angry, and deeply disappointed. My frustration was intense because my expectations had been strong. I blamed him for my pain, focusing on his behavior and the way the relationship ended.

As God began to heal my heart, He gently revealed something deeper. My frustration was not rooted solely in rejection; it was rooted in the collapse of the future I had already written in my mind. The surface issue was the breakup. The deeper issue was that my expectations had outpaced reality. I had wanted the outcome more than I wanted God's will. Once I could see that, healing began — not because the situation changed, but because my understanding did.

This principle applies far beyond relationships. Often, what frustrates us about others is not really about them; it is about what we expected from them. When those expectations go unmet, frustration sets in. But frustration is not resolved by forcing people to change. It is resolved by tracing expectations back to their source and examining whether they align with God's will or merely our own desires.

Scripture gives us examples of people who experienced real frustration and yet responded well. Nehemiah is one such example. When he learned that leaders were exploiting the poor during the rebuilding of Jerusalem, Scripture says he was very angry (Nehemiah 5:6, ESV). His frustration was justified. But instead of reacting impulsively, he paused, reflected, and addressed the issue with wisdom and restraint (Nehemiah 5:7, ESV). His frustration led to correction and restoration rather than destruction.

Hannah offers another picture. Her frustration was long-standing and deeply personal. She was barren, provoked, and misunderstood. Scripture says she was deeply distressed and poured out her soul before the Lord (1 Samuel 1:10, 15, ESV). Her circumstances did not immediately change, but her posture did. After surrendering her pain to God, her countenance changed before her situation did (1 Samuel 1:18, ESV). Surrendering to God led her to trust rather than bitterness.

David frequently expressed frustration as well, particularly in the Psalms. He questioned God, lamented injustice, and cried out in distress (Psalm 13:1, ESV). Yet when given the opportunity to act on his frustration by harming Saul, he refused, choosing instead to honor God's timing (1 Samuel 24:6, ESV). His frustration was real, but it did not govern his obedience.

The apostle Paul also encountered repeated frustration through opposition, imprisonment, and unmet expectations. In Acts 16, after being unjustly beaten and jailed, Paul and Silas responded not with outrage but with prayer and worship (Acts 16:25, ESV). Their frustration did not disappear, but it was submitted to God, and He used their response to bring deliverance and testimony.

That said, not all frustration has deep, hidden roots. Sometimes frustration is simply part of being human. It can be a traffic jam, when you left home on time, and now you are late. It can be a long line when you are tired. It can be a small disruption that comes at the wrong moment. These frustrations do not necessarily point to misplaced desires or spiritual failure. They are reminders that we live in a broken world and life happens.

Scripture reminds us that God fully understands our human limitations and weaknesses. He is not distant from our experiences, nor is He unaware of how easily we become overwhelmed by inconvenience, disappointment, or delay. Yet God Himself is never governed by irritation, loss of control, or reactive emotion. What we experience as frustration does not originate in Him, but He graciously meets us in it. Our call is not to deny what we feel, but to bring those feelings into the light of His will so that our responses are shaped by trust rather than impulse.

The challenge is that many responses we consider "normal" are not normal when measured against God's will. Sarcasm, harshness, withdrawal, or simmering resentment may feel justified, but they do not reflect the Spirit of God at work in us. God understands our humanity and meets us with grace, but growth involves learning to respond differently than what feels instinctive.

This is why tracking frustration is so important. Sometimes frustration reveals misplaced expectations that require repentance and realignment. Other times, it reveals the need for patience, grace, and dependence on God in the ordinary inconveniences of life. In both cases, frustration becomes an invitation — not to control outcomes, but to trust God more deeply.

Frustration does not have to define us. When we trace it to its source, it becomes a tool rather than a trap. God can use it to expose what needs surrender, to strengthen patience, and to deepen trust. And when we learn to track frustration honestly and humbly, we discover that it no longer has the power to control us.

Latonya Sterling

Chapter 4: Frustration at Home Marriage and Family Dynamics

Home is often the place where frustration shows up most clearly. We may be able to put on patience for coworkers, church members, or even strangers in public, but behind closed doors our true selves are revealed. Family life exposes both our strengths and our weaknesses, and marriage has a way of bringing frustrations to the surface.

One of the lessons I had to learn early in marriage was that my husband and I are two different people. I entered marriage with the understanding that I could not change him. But even though I knew that truth in my head, I still found myself trying to change him. And to make it harder, many of the things I wanted to change in him seemed like they honored God. Surely it wasn't wrong to want him to grow into a stronger man of faith. Surely it wasn't wrong to want our marriage to reflect biblical values.

Because of this, I tried to help him by nudging him in the direction I thought he should go. I placed marriage books on his nightstand, hoping he would read them and take the lead. I brought up discussions I thought would strengthen us, but the more I pressed, the further away he seemed to move — not from our marriage, but from those conversations. He wasn't abandoning me, but he was shutting down from the pressure of my expectations.

At the time, I didn't see it that way. I told myself I was helping him. I thought, *What's wrong with wanting my husband to be a better man of God?* But the truth was that I had taken on a role that didn't belong to me. What I saw as encouragement, felt like pressure to him. What I believed was godly counsel, he experienced as something being imposed on him. My frustration grew, and I blamed him for it, never realizing that much of it came from my own unwillingness to let the Holy Spirit do His work in him.

It took me years, far too many, to see the truth. But thank God, He opened my eyes before it was too late. I realized that my responsibility was not to change my husband. My responsibility was to respect him, honor him, and pray for him. Real transformation, the kind that lasts, can only be done by the Spirit of God. The Bible says, "It is God who works in you, both to will and to work for his good pleasure" (Philippians 2:13, ESV). If even my own growth is the work of the Spirit, how could I expect myself to engineer someone else's growth?

Now, more than twenty years later, I can look back and see how much has changed, not just in my husband, but in me. Many of the things that used to irritate me don't irritate me anymore, not because they disappeared, but because my perspective shifted. I no longer feel the need to fix him. I no longer see it as my job to mold him into the man I think he should be. Instead, I am learning to simply love him, pray for him, and trust God with the rest.

Marriage has taught me that frustration often comes when we try to control what belongs to God. The same is true in parenting and other family relationships. Our children, our spouses, our relatives — they are all people with their own will, their own journey, and their own relationship with God. We can teach, encourage, and pray, but we cannot determine outcomes. When we try, frustration follows. When we surrender, peace comes.

Parenting provides another picture of this same principle. There are times when we, as parents, present our children with what appears to be choices, but when they exercise that freedom in a way that opposes what we want, frustration and irritation quickly follow. In those moments, the issue is not the child's decision but the illusion of choice. We were not truly offering freedom; we were hoping for compliance. When parents respond with attitude or anger because a child chose differently, it reveals that outcome-driven authority, rather than guidance, was at the center of the interaction. Outcome-driven authority is trying to control what someone does instead of helping them grow. A choice is presented, but only one outcome is truly accepted. Frustration arises when a different decision is made. Just because we are parents does not mean we are called to govern every area of our children's lives as though they are incapable of thinking or having preferences of their own.

Healthy parenting requires discernment, not domination. There are necessities of life where parental authority must be exercised, but there are also areas where flexibility and respect are appropriate. Even something as simple as choosing where the family eats can become a lesson in honoring others. If I want to go to a restaurant my children genuinely dislike, forcing them to go and endure food they do not enjoy serves no real purpose. It only communicates that their preferences do not matter.

Likewise, as children grow, their age and maturity must be considered. With a seventeen-year-old and a thirteen-year-old living at home, I am not going to drag them along to activities like getting my hair or nails done if they do not want to go. Acknowledging appropriate autonomy does not weaken parental authority; it strengthens trust. Good parenting is not about forcing compliance in nonessential matters, but about guiding children with wisdom, respect, and love.

Many parents, out of love, want to give their children what they never had. If they were never able to play sports, join clubs, or pursue certain talents, they sometimes push their children into those activities to make up for it. On the surface, this can sound noble: *I just want my child to be well-rounded.* But if the child is not interested, or if the activity is not suited to their gifts, it can quickly become a source of frustration for both parent and child. Instead of enjoying the activity, the child feels pressured, and instead of celebrating who the child truly is, the parent feels disappointed. The issue is not that sports or extracurricular activities are wrong. They can be wonderful. The issue is when a parent's personal longing is projected onto their child, turning a gift of opportunity into a burden of expectation. The Apostle Paul addressed this very dynamic when he wrote, "Fathers, do not provoke your children to anger, but bring them up in the discipline and instruction of the Lord" (Ephesians 6:4, ESV). To provoke is to stir up irritation, resentment, or discouragement. And often, what provokes children most is not healthy discipline but unrealistic or misplaced parental expectations.

Family frustrations also surface in relationships with in-laws. I have always gotten along with mine, but there was a season when things became rocky with my mother-in-law. It wasn't that I had done anything to her or that she had intentionally wronged me. The tension arose when we were dealing with an issue concerning one of my daughters. My mother-in-law thought she was being helpful by giving her perspective, but my husband and I chose a different approach. Because we didn't follow her advice, there was frustration. It would have been easy for that frustration to harden into division, but the Lord showed us how to resolve it. In the end, we learned that unity in marriage sometimes means graciously disagreeing with family and still choosing love over conflict.

Even sibling relationships can be a source of frustration. Siblings often become so familiar with one another that respect is set aside. Hurtful jokes, belittling comments, or constant bickering can be brushed off as *normal* — "that's just how brothers and sisters are." What the world calls normal, God does not. Looking back, I sometimes think about how I could have been a better example to my younger siblings. Instead of letting frustration dictate my responses, I could have shown them love, patience, and respect. That's why I treasure the advice of my mentor, Dad Dotson, who once told me, *"Don't let your kids fuss and fight with each other. The world says it's normal, but to God it is not."* His words reminded me that even sibling dynamics need training and intentionality. My kids were not perfect, but rarely did I hear sibling arguments in my household with my daughters. My sons get along well.

Parents often get frustrated with their children's behavior without realizing that they themselves allowed certain patterns to go unchecked. When children are left to argue, disrespect, or fight, those behaviors grow. Then, when they escalate, parents blame the child without recognizing that a lack of correction played a part. Proverbs 22:6 tells us, "Train up a child in the way he should go; even when he is old he will not depart from it." This is a wise saying, not a biblical promise. It doesn't remove human choice or override responsibility. It affirms the importance and influence of intentional training We live in a society today where so many parents are not training their children. Instead, teachers, coaches, and even strangers in public settings are left to deal with behaviors that should have been addressed at home. This cycle produces frustration not only for parents, but for everyone else around their children. God's Word calls us as parents to take responsibility, not to provoke, neglect, or excuse, but to guide our children with love and discipline. A major part of this guidance is what we model in our own behavior.

Whether in marriage, parenting, in-laws, or sibling relationships, the truth is the same: frustration grows when we project our standards, push for control, or ignore our role in training. Peace comes when we surrender outcomes to God, respect one another, and honor His design for family.

Chapter 5: Frustration at Work
Learning to Trust God in the Workplace

Work can be one of the greatest testing grounds for frustration. Deadlines, coworkers, bosses, and job descriptions all carry expectations, and when those expectations aren't met, irritation follows quickly. Sometimes we blame company culture. Sometimes we blame our supervisors. Other times we blame our workload. But as with family and marriage, frustration at work often reveals something deeper inside us.

I remember a season when I worked as a secretary in an office. My direct supervisor was another woman in the department, and she often came to me with tasks that had been assigned to her. But instead of saying, I need you to do this for me, she would say, "We need to do this." The problem was that "we" always seemed to end up being "me." Task after task landed in my lap, and I grew increasingly frustrated. I felt like she was dumping her responsibilities on me, and the more I thought about it, the more frustrated I became.

In time, the Lord showed me the truth. My frustration wasn't about her. It was about me. I hadn't yet understood what it meant to serve. The work she gave me was within my skill set and my job description. I could do it, and I was being paid to support the department. The problem wasn't the tasks themselves. It was my perspective. I didn't like the way she framed it, as if we were doing it together, when I was the one executing the work. But if I had looked at it through the lens of service, I would have seen an opportunity to strengthen the team, lighten her load, and grow in humility.

That realization stung at first, but it freed me. Jesus said, "Whoever would be great among you must be your servant, and whoever would be first among you must be your slave, even as the Son of Man came not to be served but to serve, and to give his life as a ransom for many" (Matthew 20:26–28, ESV). Serving others is not about keeping score. It's not about whether the workload feels "fair." It's about reflecting Christ, who laid aside His rights and gave Himself for us. My frustration came from clinging to my sense of fairness instead of embracing God's call to serve.

Another experience brought this lesson home even more deeply. I once worked for a supervisor who specifically told me she was training me to move into her position when she relocated with her family. I was excited about the opportunity and worked hard, believing I was being groomed for a promotion. But when one of her old friends returned to the company and was rehired, everything changed. My supervisor shifted her attention from training me to training her friend. When she eventually left, the position I thought was mine went to someone else.

I was disappointed, hurt, and irritated. I found myself resenting the young woman who had been given what I felt should have been mine. For a long time, I was so annoyed just being around her. But as the Lord began to deal with my heart, I realized the real issue wasn't her — it was me. If that position was meant for me, God would have given it to me. Instead,

He was using the situation to expose jealousy, resentment, and a lack of trust in His sovereignty. My frustration revealed that I was more focused on what I thought I deserved than on God's plan for me.

The story didn't end there. I was eventually fired from that job over an accusation that wasn't even true. At first it felt devastating, but I chose to trust God's hand in it. That closed door led me into a new job that became the very path God used to move me into ministry. What looked like a setback was really a setup for His greater purpose.

This experience taught me that what feels like being passed over or mistreated can be God's way of redirecting us. Psalm 75:6–7 reminds us, "For not from the east or from the west and not from the wilderness comes lifting up, but it is God who executes judgment, putting down one and lifting up another" (ESV). In the life of a believer, promotion does not come from people. It comes from God.

I want to say this carefully: I believe racism is real. Prejudice and bias exist, and they can create real obstacles. But as born-again believers, we must never forget that God's sovereignty overrules even the brokenness of human systems. Revelation 3:7 declares that Christ "opens and no one will shut, who shuts and no one opens" (ESV). When our trust is in God rather than in people, systems, or history, we can walk in confidence that no one, regardless of their character flaws or prejudices, can block what God has ordained for us.

Beyond personal stories, workplace frustrations can take many forms. Sometimes it's the coworker who constantly complains or stirs up drama, making the environment toxic. Other times it's the manager who micromanages every detail, leaving you feeling suffocated. For some, it's the disappointment of being overlooked for promotion after years of dedication. For others, it's feeling stuck in a job that doesn't fit their gifts or passion, wondering if their work has any purpose at all.

In all of these cases, frustration grows when we focus only on what others are doing or not doing. The reality is, workplaces are filled with imperfect people — including us. No office, team, or company is without flaws. But when our hearts anchor in the truth that "whatever you do, work heartily, as for the Lord and not for men" (Colossians 3:23, ESV), frustration loses its grip. We begin to see that our true Boss is Christ Himself, and He never overlooks our labor.

Work frustration often comes down to perspective. We think our career should move faster, our coworkers should be kinder, our bosses should be wiser. Sometimes those expectations are fair, but even when they aren't met, God calls us to faithfulness. When we serve Him in our work, we can trust Him to use every task, every delay, and even every disappointment to shape us for His purpose.

In the end, frustration at work reminds us that the workplace is not just about paychecks and promotions. It can be a classroom where God teaches us humility, patience, and trust. Every assignment, every conflict, every closed door is an opportunity to surrender our expectations and align our hearts with His will. When we see work through that lens, frustration

Frustration

is no longer a wall. It becomes a window into God's greater plan. Even the seasons that feel stagnant or unfair are not wasted in His hands. God uses what frustrates us to refine our character, redirect our steps, and quietly prepare us for what is next. When we allow Him to reshape our perspective, the very place that once felt like a burden can become the place where deeper trust and lasting transformation are formed.

Latonya Sterling

Chapter 6: Frustration in the Church When Spiritual Expectations Collide

Church is one of those places where some might expect frustration to be rare. After all, if anywhere should be filled with peace and unity, surely it would be the house of God. Yet in many ways, church can be one of the most frustrating places of all. Why? Because as believers, our expectations for one another are often very high. We assume that since we are the children of God, everything should be in order, everyone should be in harmony, and no one should disappoint us. But the reality is that the church is made up of people—saved, yes, but still growing, still human, and still learning to walk in step with the Spirit.

Frustration in the church often does not come from unhealthy leadership or unloving people. More often, it flows from something much more subtle: the unintentional transfer of personal spiritual convictions onto others as though they are universal commands from God. Many of us discover certain practices that deeply nurture our walk with the Lord. Those practices become life-giving for us—and they should. But, without realizing it, we can begin to treat what has become meaningful for us as though it must be mandatory for everyone else. This is rarely done with harmful intent but often flows from a genuine desire for others to experience the same spiritual fruit we have found. Yet good intentions alone do not make a personal conviction universal.

Spiritual disciplines are personal practices that help believers grow in intimacy with God, sensitivity to His Spirit, and maturity in Christ. They are not tools for earning God's favor, but responses to His grace. They are ways we place ourselves in positions to be shaped by His presence.

Common spiritual disciplines include prayer, reading and meditating on Scripture, fasting, worship, fellowship with other believers, giving, serving, and Sabbath rest. Each of these disciplines can be life-giving and deeply transformative. While all believers are called to spiritual growth, the expression of that growth may look different from person to person and season to season. Spiritual disciplines are invitations, not measuring sticks. They are tools for formation, not instruments of comparison. What strengthens one person in a particular rhythm may not look exactly the same for another, especially across different seasons of life. When spiritual practices move from being personal responses to God into unspoken expectations placed on others, they can quietly become sources of frustration.

Frustration can arise in leadership just as it does in every other area of life, but the presence of frustration does not mean something is wrong with leadership itself. It simply reveals the same human tendencies that exist in all believers — expectations, assumptions, and differing perspectives that must continually be brought before God. Leadership does not remove a person from the need for surrender; it actually deepens it.

One of the most helpful things I have learned is that the spiritual disciplines that sustain a believer's life with God were never meant to begin at leadership. Prayer, time in the Word, worship, and fellowship are not leadership requirements; they are foundational practices for all believers. When this is understood, leadership no longer becomes the place where spiritual pressure begins, but simply another place where faith is lived out. This perspective alone removes a great deal of unnecessary frustration because it anchors a leader's identity in being a child of God rather than in holding a role.

As leaders, frustration often surfaces when expectations are unclear, unspoken, or misaligned. But instead of allowing that frustration to settle into irritation or discouragement, leaders are invited to examine what lies beneath it. Am I frustrated because someone expects something unreasonable of me or because I feel misunderstood? Am I frustrated because I disagree with a responsibility or because I have not yet communicated my concerns? These moments become opportunities not for resentment, but for maturity.

This is where Colossians 3:23–24 (ESV) becomes especially important for leadership: "Whatever you do, work heartily, as for the Lord and not for men, knowing that from the Lord you will receive the inheritance as your reward. You are serving the Lord Christ." When leadership is anchored in serving God rather than seeking affirmation, agreement, or validation from people, frustration loses much of its power. Leaders are free to serve faithfully without being governed by how their efforts are received or interpreted.

I also had to confront frustration in myself when I realized I was imposing my personal ways of doing things on others in ministry. I expected people to serve, communicate, and function according to my methods, assuming because something worked for me, it should work for them as well. When they did not respond or perform in the way I expected, I became frustrated, not realizing that I was quietly hindering their growth by limiting them to my perspective. It was only through the Holy Spirit's correction that I began to see that I was requiring preference where God had only required obedience. Once I surrendered my methods to God instead of expecting others to conform to them, both my frustration and their freedom in ministry began to change.

When expectations feel burdensome, one of the most spiritually healthy responses is not withdrawal or silent frustration, but humble communication and surrender. Scripture shows us that peace within the body is preserved not by silence, but by clarity and love. Ephesians 4:2–3 (ESV) instructs believers to walk "with all humility and gentleness, with patience, bearing with one another in love, eager to maintain the unity of the Spirit in the bond of peace." Many frustrations dissolve not through endurance alone, but through understanding grounded in humility.

Another key to resolving leadership frustration is remembering that people, even leaders, will not always see things the same way. Differences in perspective are not failures of faith; they are part of being human. When we accept that others may think differently without being wrong or ungodly, we are freed from needing everyone to agree with us to walk in peace. This posture protects leaders from unnecessary frustration by keeping trust in God rather than in uniformity of thought.

Frustration is not limited to leaders; pastors also experience it, not because they are weak or unspiritual, but because they love people deeply in a fallen world. Pastors often carry the emotional weight of praying for people, teaching truth, walking alongside brokenness, and still watching individuals make choices that lead to pain. Others feel the strain of being expected to be endlessly accessible, emotionally steady, and spiritually strong without rest or margin. Still others may quietly wrestle with feeling unseen or overlooked, not because they seek recognition, but because deep investment carries emotional weight and moments of invisibility can feel isolating even in faithful service.

These experiences, while they can cause frustration, can also become invitations to surrender. They invite pastors to continually place their labor before God rather than before human response. Pastors are not called to carry people, but to love people, trusting the Holy Spirit to do the transforming work. When pastors remain *rooted in God's love* rather than human response, frustration no longer has authority to harden the heart or distort the calling.

God never intended pastors to carry the full weight of spiritual care alone. Scripture presents the church as one body with many members, each supplying what they have been given (1 Corinthians 12:12–27, ESV). When responsibility is shared, when believers take ownership of their own spiritual growth, and when leaders are supported rather than overextended, frustration gives way to sustainability and joy.

Ultimately, leadership frustration is resolved the same way all frustration is resolved — by bringing expectations, assumptions, and emotions into the light of God's will. When leaders and pastors refuse to internalize frustration and instead surrender it to God, frustration loses its power to shape attitudes or decisions. Leadership then becomes not a place where pressure builds, but a place where grace is practiced and maturity is formed.

Chapter 7: God Is Not Like Us
Why We Can't Project Human Irritation onto Him

One of the most comforting truths in Scripture is that God is not like us. While human beings are often impatient, irritable, or quick to judge, God is steady, faithful, and abounding in love. Where we can be tossed about by emotions, He remains constant. Where we may react in frustration, He responds with mercy. This contrast matters deeply, because the way we see God shapes the way we handle our own frustrations.

Scripture makes this distinction clear. "For my thoughts are not your thoughts, neither are your ways my ways, declares the Lord. For as the heavens are higher than the earth, so are my ways higher than your ways and my thoughts than your thoughts" (Isaiah 55:8–9, ESV). God's perspective is infinitely higher than ours. Where we see only a moment, He sees the beginning and the end. Where we are moved by pressure, He is guided by purpose. Where our discipline is often reactive, His is always rooted in love.

When we read stories of God's judgment in the Bible, it can be tempting to interpret them through the lens of human frustration. For example, when Israel rebelled in the wilderness, we might picture God as a parent who has finally "had enough" and explodes in anger. But God's actions are never reactionary. His discipline is not rooted in irritation but in holiness and love. Hebrews 12:10–11 explains, "He disciplines us for our good, that we may share his holiness. For the moment all discipline seems painful rather than pleasant, but later it yields the peaceful fruit of righteousness to those who have been trained by it" (ESV). God's correction is never about venting frustration. It is always about producing fruit.

This is a sharp contrast to how we handle frustration. When Moses struck the rock instead of speaking to it (Numbers 20:10–12, ESV), his reaction flowed from irritation with the people. His anger caused him to misrepresent God's character before Israel. Instead of seeing God's mercy and provision, the people witnessed Moses' frustration. That moment stands as a reminder: when we project our human responses onto God, we risk painting Him as harsh, impatient, or unstable, when in reality He is faithful, merciful, and steadfast.

This is one of the reasons I try to be very careful when teaching in church. It can be tempting to impose how I think God feels or what I imagine He might be thinking in a certain situation, especially when using humor to make Him seem more relatable. But the truth is, I don't know exactly what God is thinking when He watches someone's behavior, and I don't know precisely what He is feeling in a given moment. What I do know, because Scripture makes it clear, is that He is loving, kind, merciful, and that He disciplines those He loves (Hebrews 12:6, ESV). So, I resist the urge to apply my personal perspective as a parent or leader to how God operates. To do so risks shrinking His holiness down to the limits of my human thinking.

One of the clearest demonstrations of God's character is found in how He describes Himself to Moses: "The Lord, the Lord, a God merciful and gracious, slow to anger, and abounding in steadfast love and faithfulness" (Exodus 34:6, ESV). Notice the difference. Human beings are quick to anger and slow to let go of offenses. But God is slow to anger and abounding in love. Even His anger is not like ours. It is righteous, just, and perfectly measured.

When we carry frustration into our view of God, it often produces fear. We begin to see Him as someone who is easily provoked, constantly disappointed, or waiting for us to fail. But Scripture tells us, "There is therefore now no condemnation for those who are in Christ Jesus" (Romans 8:1, ESV). God does not look at His children with irritation. He looks at us through the finished work of Christ. His discipline is not punishment for punishment's sake, but loving correction that draws us back to Him.

Understanding this truth changes how we handle our own frustrations. Instead of excusing our irritability as "just being human," we can hold it up to the light of God's nature. Where we might respond with impatience, He responds with mercy. Where we might give up on people, He remains faithful. Where we might allow bitterness to grow, He continues to pursue in love. As we grow in Him, the Spirit transforms us so that our responses reflect His heart rather than our flesh.

This doesn't mean we will never feel frustration. We are human, and God understands our weaknesses. But it does mean that frustration does not have to define us, nor does it have to dictate our choices. The more clearly we see that God is not like us, the more hope we have that we can be conformed to His image rather than trapped in our own.

At the end of the day, the most freeing truth about frustration is this: God is not like us. He does not fly off the handle, hold grudges, or stew in irritation. He is merciful, gracious, slow to anger, and abounding in steadfast love. That is why I try not to impose my own feelings on Him when I teach. I may not know exactly what God is thinking in every situation, but I do know who He is, because His Word tells me. The more clearly I see Him for who He truly is, the more I can trust Him with my own frustrations. Instead of projecting my humanity onto God, I can allow His divine character to reshape me.

As I continue to grow in my understanding of who God is, I'm learning that seeing His character clearly not only transforms my frustrations—it shapes how I interpret His actions. If God is truly slow to anger, rich in mercy, and constant in love, then even the moments in Scripture that look severe must be viewed through that same lens. His discipline cannot be separated from His heart. And that reality raises an important question: *If God is not like us in His patience or His perspective, then how should we understand the way He corrects His children?* Based on His character and nature, it stands to reason that His discipline flows from the same steadfast love that sets Him apart from us.

Chapter 8: The Flood, the Wilderness, and the Temple – God's Discipline as Love

If there is one theme that consistently challenges our view of God, it is discipline. Because we sometimes discipline out of frustration, irritation, or weariness, we assume God must do the same. But the Bible makes it clear: His discipline is never rooted in human irritation. It is always purposeful, measured, and rooted in love. When we look at major moments of judgment in Scripture — the flood, Israel's wilderness journey, and even the destruction of the temple — we see not a God lashing out in anger, but a God acting with justice and mercy to accomplish His purposes.

Take the flood, for example. Genesis tells us, "The Lord saw that the wickedness of man was great in the earth, and that every intention of the thoughts of his heart was only evil continually" (Genesis 6:5, ESV). God's response was not petty annoyance at human imperfection, but righteous judgment on a world corrupted by violence and sin. And yet even in judgment, there was mercy. Noah found favor in the eyes of the Lord (Genesis 6:8, ESV), and through him God preserved humanity. The flood shows us that God's discipline is not like human frustration — it is holy justice paired with redeeming love.

The same is true in the wilderness. After rescuing Israel from Egypt with mighty signs and wonders, God led them toward the Promised Land. But when fear overtook their faith, the people rebelled, refusing to enter the land He had promised. Numbers 14:22–23 records God's verdict: "None of the men who have seen my glory and my signs that I did in Egypt and in the wilderness, and yet have put me to the test these ten times and have not obeyed my voice, shall see the land that I swore to give to their fathers" (ESV). At first glance, this might sound like God simply ran out of patience. But in reality, His decision preserved the next generation from inheriting the unbelief of their parents. Scripture later confirms this: Judges 2:7 describes that next generation as one who "served the Lord all the days of Joshua," demonstrating that they did not repeat the rebellion of their parents but instead walked in faith under Joshua's leadership. Even in discipline, God was faithful—He remained with them for forty years, feeding them with manna, providing water from the rock, and guiding them with His presence. His discipline was not abandonment but correction, training His people to trust Him.

The destruction of the temple in Jerusalem carries a similar message. When Israel persisted in idolatry and injustice despite repeated warnings from the prophets, God allowed Babylon to conquer Jerusalem and destroy the temple (2 Kings 25:8–10, ESV). This was not the same generation that entered the Promised Land under Joshua, but a later generation who had drifted from God's commands. From a human perspective, it may have looked like God had finally "had enough" and walked away. But the prophets reveal otherwise. God was not venting irritation. He was removing false security. Through Jeremiah, God confronted this very attitude: "Do not trust in these deceptive words, 'This is the temple of the Lord, the temple of the Lord, the temple of the Lord'" (Jeremiah 7:4, ESV), exposing how the people had begun to treat the temple as a guarantee of His favor while ignoring His commands. By allowing the temple to fall, God reminded them that His presence was never confined to a building, but to a covenant relationship.

This same truth is later affirmed in the New Testament when Paul declares, "The God who made the world and everything in it, being Lord of heaven and earth, does not live in temples made by man, nor is He served by human hands, as though He needed anything" (Acts 17:24–25, ESV). Paul was teaching that God is not confined by, dependent upon, or contained within human structures. He is self-sufficient, sovereign, and relational — present with His people not because of buildings, but because of covenant.

Even in exile, He promised restoration: "For I know the plans I have for you, declares the Lord, plans for welfare and not for evil, to give you a future and a hope" (Jeremiah 29:11, ESV). And while many now apply this verse broadly, it was originally a prophetic word spoken through Jeremiah specifically to Israel in exile, assuring them that God had not abandoned His covenant or His intentions toward His people.

Under the new covenant, this truth is brought even closer. God no longer dwells among His people through stone and structure, but within them through His Spirit. Believers themselves have become His dwelling place. This means God is honored not by a particular building, but by hearts and lives that walk in covenant with Him — wherever His people gather.

Each of these moments — the flood, the wilderness, and the temple — shows us the same truth. God's discipline is not like ours. It is not the overflow of irritation or the snap of impatience. It is the steady hand of a loving Father who corrects for the sake of life. As I stated earlier, Hebrews 12:6 says it plainly: "For the Lord disciplines the one he loves, and chastises every son whom he receives" (ESV). His goal is not to crush but to restore, not to harm but to heal, not to destroy but to redeem.

When we confuse God's discipline with human frustration, we misrepresent His heart. Our irritation often springs from wounded pride, unmet expectations, or personal inconvenience. God's discipline flows from holiness and love, with eternity in view. He sees what we cannot see, and He works in ways we would never choose in order to accomplish what we most deeply need.

The flood reminds us that God takes sin seriously, but also that He provides salvation. The wilderness shows us that unbelief has consequences, but also that God never abandons His people. The temple's destruction warns us not to trust in outward forms but also points us to God's promise of restoration. In every case, His discipline is an expression of His covenant love.

When we think of discipline, we must remember that God is not like us. He does not act from irritation or impatience. His judgments are holy, His corrections are purposeful, and His love never fails. Where we might discipline to release frustration, He disciplines to produce righteousness. When we embrace this truth, frustration loses its power over us, because we learn to see correction not as rejection, but as evidence that we are His beloved children.

Latonya Sterling

Chapter 9: Faith Over Frustration
Surrendering Expectations

Surrender is one of the most challenging words in the life of a believer, yet it is also one of the most freeing. By definition, surrender means to yield control, to give up striving, to place oneself under the authority of another. In our relationship with God, surrender is not about defeat but about trust. It is the posture of letting go of our expectations and submitting our will to His, believing that His ways are higher and His plans are better.

Jesus Himself gave us the clearest picture of surrender in the garden of Gethsemane. On the night before His crucifixion, He prayed, "Father, if you are willing, remove this cup from me. Nevertheless, not my will, but yours, be done" (Luke 22:42, ESV). In that moment, surrender did not erase the weight of His anguish, but it aligned His heart with the Father's will. True surrender is not pretending we are unbothered by disappointment or pain. It is choosing to trust God's will above our own even in the midst of it.

When we talk about frustration, most of it comes down to our attachment to outcomes. We want people to behave a certain way. We want circumstances to follow our plan. We want life to bend to our expectations. And when those things don't happen, frustration rises. Surrender interrupts that cycle. Instead of clinging to outcomes we were never meant to manage, surrender places them in the hands of Jesus. Instead of demanding that our will be done, surrender echoes His prayer: *Not my will, but Yours.*

This shift changes everything. Abraham had to surrender his timeline when God delayed the promise of Isaac for decades. Joseph had to surrender his dreams to God's process while unjustly imprisoned in Egypt. David had to surrender his desire for the throne while hiding in caves from Saul. None of them got what they expected when they wanted it. Yet each discovered that God's timing and God's way were perfect. Their surrender turned potential frustration into fertile ground for faith.

Romans 8:28 anchors this truth: "And we know that for those who love God all things work together for good, for those who are called according to his purpose" (ESV). Surrender means believing this even when we cannot see how it will work. It means trusting that every closed door, every delay, and every disappointment is not wasted, but woven into God's sovereign plan.

This doesn't mean surrender is easy. Our flesh resists letting go. Our pride wants control. Our hearts crave certainty. Even Jesus sweat drops of blood as He surrendered in the garden (Luke 22:44, ESV). But on the other side of surrender is peace. Philippians 4:6–7 promises that when we bring our anxieties to God in prayer, His peace, which surpasses all understanding, will guard our hearts and minds in Christ Jesus.

This is an ongoing learning process for me in my life. Times when I tried to manage outcomes, I found myself drowning in frustration, resentment, and weariness. But when

I laid those outcomes before God, in my marriage, in parenting, in work, in ministry, peace returned. Not because everything instantly changed, but because my heart shifted from striving to trusting. The moment I surrendered, frustration began to lose its grip. I'm not professing that I no longer get irritated. But, frustration does not guide my decisions nearly as much as it used to.

Paul described it simply: "For we walk by faith, not by sight" (2 Corinthians 5:7, ESV). Walking by sight means leaning on what we can see, measure, and predict. Walking by faith means releasing control, even when we don't understand, and trusting God's unseen hand because experientially and through His Word we know He is trustworthy and faithful. Trusting God is not a passive mindset but an active dependence. It means we rely upon Him, seek His wisdom, receive the answers we need, and walk it out by His enabling power. Our acts of obedience and trust are not attempts to earn His favor but responses to His love, already demonstrated toward us in Christ (Romans 5:8, ESV). We must know beyond a shadow of a doubt that God loves us, cares for us, and knows what is best for us. The challenge comes because our flesh resists surrender. It wants its own way, regardless of how good and faithful God has been. But when we anchor ourselves in His love, trust becomes possible, and faith becomes more than belief in our heads; it becomes the daily application of reliance on Him.

Surrender is not weakness. It is strength rooted in trust. It is laying down our expectations and choosing to believe that

God's sovereignty is greater than our own plans. Faith over frustration means echoing Jesus' words, *Not my will, but Yours be done.* It means exchanging the weight of unmet expectations for the peace of resting in His plan. And when we choose surrender, we find that the very places where frustration once ruled become the very places where God's grace shines the brightest.

Conclusion: Living Beyond Frustration

Frustration is a reality of life, but it doesn't have to rule your life. Every story in this book — from Moses at the rock to Jonah outside Nineveh, from Naaman's anger to Israel's wilderness wanderings — reminds us that frustration often exposes something deeper. It reveals where our expectations have collided with reality, where our standards have been projected onto others, or where our desire for control has overshadowed trust in God.

The challenge is clear: Will you allow frustration to push you toward bitterness, irritation, and wrong choices? Or will you let it be the signal that drives you to surrender and trust? Every time frustration rises, you have an opportunity — not to suppress it, not to excuse it, but to trace it back to its root and release it to God.

The encouragement is this: You do not walk this journey alone. God has given you His Spirit to guide, strengthen, and empower you. He has already proven His love at the cross. He has already secured your future in Christ. He has already promised His peace to those who trust Him. You don't have to fight frustration in your own strength. You can rest in the God who is merciful, gracious, and abounding in steadfast love.

As you close this book, I challenge you to take one area of frustration in your life right now and lay it before the Lord. Ask Him to show you what lies beneath it. Surrender your expectations, your desire to manage outcomes, your personal standards, and your fear. Trust Him, not just with words, but with action, by walking in obedience and reliance on His enabling power.

Closing Prayer

Father, I pray for the one reading these words. Where frustration has weighed them down, replace it with Your peace. Where disappointment has clouded their heart, remind them of Your faithful love. Teach them to surrender their expectations into Your hands, not with fear but with trust, knowing You are good and wise in all that You do. Strengthen their faith to rely on You daily, not just in thought but in action, walking in obedience by Your Spirit's power. And when their flesh resists, remind them that Your grace is sufficient, and Your love never fails. May their life be a testimony that frustration does not have the final word — You do. In Jesus' name, Amen.

Special Acknowledgement

One of the commitments I have made as a writer is to invite at least one trusted voice to read my work before it is published. This practice serves as a form of accountability, allowing me to consider how my words may impact others beyond my own perspective. Because of her shepherd's heart and spiritual discernment, I entrusted this manuscript to my pastor, Denise Wheeler.

Her thoughtful insight and willingness to take time to gather clarity helped me recognize where a section of this book had drifted from what I believe was God's true intent. During that pause—while waiting for her input—God was also at work, gently speaking to my heart and redirecting my focus. What could have remained a place of frustration became an opportunity for growth, reflection, and deeper alignment with His purpose.

This book is not meant to magnify frustration, but to point readers toward God in the midst of it. I am deeply grateful to Pastor Denise for creating space for that pause, for her wisdom, and for her role in helping this message remain rooted in grace and truth.

Works Cited

The Holy Bible, English Standard Version. Wheaton, IL: Crossway Bibles, 2016.

Merriam-Webster's Collegiate Dictionary, 11th ed. Springfield, MA: Merriam-Webster, 2020.

Previous Works

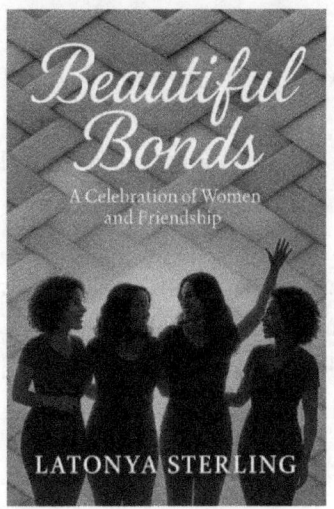

Coming Soon

In *Forgiven to Forgive: How the Finished Work of Christ Frees the Heart*, I explore one of the most misunderstood and emotionally charged teachings in the Christian faith—forgiveness. This short but powerful book gently reframes forgiveness through the lens of grace, helping readers understand that forgiveness is not a burden to earn God's love, but a freedom that flows from knowing we are already forgiven in Christ. With biblical clarity, practical wisdom, and compassionate insight, *Forgiven to Forgive* invites readers into healing, emotional safety, and spiritual freedom rooted in the finished work of Jesus.

www.ingramcontent.com/pod-product-compliance
Lightning Source LLC
LaVergne TN
LVHW051201080426
835508LV00021B/2751